CREATIVE**SHRED** **GUITAR**EXERCISES

100 Advanced Shred Exercises to Enhance your Creative Guitar Chops

CHRIS**ZOUPA**

FUNDAMENTAL**CHANGES**

Creative Shred Guitar Exercises

100 Advanced Shred Exercises to Enhance your Creative Guitar Chops

ISBN: 978-1-78933-222-3

Published by **www.fundamental-changes.com**

Edited by Joseph Alexander and Tim Pettingale

www.fundamental-changes.com

Over 12,000 fans on Facebook: **FundamentalChangesInGuitar**

Instagram: **FundamentalChanges**

For over 350 Free Guitar Lessons with Videos Check Out

www.fundamental-changes.com

Cover Image Copyright: *Artwork for Electric Bears*

Contents

Introduction   4

Get the Audio   5

Chapter One: Epic Picking for the Discerning Time Traveller (Warm-ups and Preliminary Pick Shreds)   6
Picking Warm-ups   6
Pentatonic Shreds   12
Diatonic & Harmonic Shreds… Incoming blisters!   17
Picking with Arpeggios   20
Stutter Picking   24
A Gentleman's Conclusion to Picking   26

Chapter Two: Legato for Self Defence   27
Warm-up Legato   27
Badass Pentatonic Legato   32
Deadly Diatonic Legato   36
Legato Arpeggios… Is That Even a Thing?!   40
Messaen Diminished & Melodic Minor Legato   43
Hammer-ons From Nowhere   46
Smoother & Weirder: A Smooth Summation   49

Chapter Three: Arpeggios and Crazy Sweeps   50
Warm-up Nonsense Sweeps   50
Upgrade Your Three-String Sweeps   52
Level Up Your Five-String Sweeps   60
Change Your Six-String Sweep Game   64
Building Sweeps   67
Revenge of the Janitor: Sweeps & Reflections   71

Chapter Four: Outlandish Tapping   72
Warm-up Taps   72
Pentatonic Taps for Snazzy Ladies & Gentleman   75
Diabolic Diatonic Taps   79
Exotic Taps (Let's Get Sassy)   82
Advanced Tapped Arpeggios   85
Expressive Taps: How to Tap… With Your Heart on Your Sleeve   93

Epilogue & Acknowledgments   96

Introduction

'Twas a warm Christmas morning as I sat by the fire, brandy in hand, when an epiphany suddenly occurred to me:

I must write a new guide to creative shred guitar... and it must be more insane, more ridiculous, more outlandish... and more rock!

It's possible that I just needed an excuse to commission yet more indulgent artwork of myself in a variety of hilarious steampunk situations. But aside from that noble cause, there are some awesome guitar ideas I want to teach you too.

I got busy and wrote down my best shred guitar exercises – legato drills, sweep sequences and tapping concepts – that were outright outlandish. And it is with great excitement that I finally get to share these ideas with you. The goal of this book is to get you thinking outside of the box and help you break out of your rut!

This book can be used as a standalone bible of shred, but it picks up where *Ultimate Shred Machine* left off. Essentially, we're going to take your guitar skills, blend them into a frozen yoghurt smoothie, mix it up with a Long Island iced tea, then throw you on a rollercoaster.

So, sit back, put your shred cap on, and enjoy some of the weirdest, coolest, least-beige exercises I've ever created.

Zoups

Get the Audio

The audio files for this book are available to download for free from **www.fundamental-changes.com.** The link is in the top right-hand corner. Simply select this book title from the drop-down menu and follow the instructions to get the audio.

We recommend that you download the files directly to your computer, not to your tablet, and extract them there before adding them to your media library. You can then put them on your tablet, iPod or burn them to CD. On the download page there is a help PDF and we also provide technical support via the contact form.

For over 350 Free Guitar Lessons with Videos Check out:

www.fundamental-changes.com

Over 12,000 fans on Facebook: **FundamentalChangesInGuitar**

Instagram: **FundamentalChanges**

Chapter One: Epic Picking for the Discerning Time Traveller (Warm-ups and Preliminary Pick Shreds)

When the common gentleman thinks of shredding, it is often reduced to things like picking efficiency and the role that plays in the cleanliness of our phrases and execution of our ideas. Therefore, it's no mystery as to why I insist on beginning this journey in the town of shred from the get-go.

It's very easy to get caught up in the meat and veg world of monotonous diatonic shredding and fall back on exercises you found on a 1993 VHS instructional guitar video (starring a guitarist whose name you don't remember, who was in a band that had one and a half good songs). Don't worry, we won't do that – this book is all about creativity. The exercises and examples here will take you to some outlandish extremes.

We're going to start this chapter with a few warm-up ideas. Partly to get some blood circulating in those fingers but mainly to tell your brain, "It's shredding time!"

Picking Warm-ups

A good warm-up routine is the best way to jump start your playing and get the most out of your practice sessions.

Personally, I'm a huge advocate of chromatic, whole-tone and whacky atonal shred ideas in my warm-ups because the melodic content of these scales is intentionally not pleasing to the ear. This means it's perfectly acceptable to play everything like a robot and concentrate 100% on your technique and execution.

The first exercise in this section uses a chromatic pattern that works diagonally across the fretboard. Use all four fingers and try to keep the picking speed and volume consistent.

Example 1a:

In Example 1b, you'll play a combination of descending and ascending chromatic and diminished arpeggios. This approach will outline a diminished arpeggio idea, without sounding too much like Rimsky-Korsakov or Slayer.

This exercise is geared at building finger independence with four-note-per-string chromatics. It will also get you crossing strings quickly with diminished arpeggios.

Example 1b:

Next, move on to Example 1c. It contains tritone, major 7th and augmented chord shapes to crawl across the fretboard to build independence and coordination.

Example 1c:

In the next example you'll take the chord shapes above and play them with alternating string skips. Feel free to use both alternate and hybrid picking as both skills will become useful later.

Example 1d:

The next exercise uses the whole tone scale in six-note groupings, ascending then descending.

This nonsense scale will help you to focus on building speed and confidence without the scale needing to sound nice. Let's face it, the whole tone scale is about as sonically appealing as Yoko Ono singing Rammstein.[1]

Example 1e:

---

1. The opinions of Chris Zoupa are his own and in no way reflect the opinions of Fundamental Changes Ltd. Sorry Yoko.

The next exercise helps to build your *outside picking*. Start on an upstroke to ensure you're always picking outside-to-in. This will help you to play less linear melodic sequences and build your dexterity.

Example 1f:

Next, the ideas from the previous examples have been modified to confound you with the addition of a string skip. "Why?" you may ask. Firstly, because string skipping is a totally badass technique, but more importantly it helps to add crazy, unpredictable intervals into your playing.

Example 1g:

Pentatonic Shreds

The pentatonic scale is the trusted scale of Blues, Rock and Metal players. It's kind of like hiring Mark Wahlberg to be in your film. He can do everything from heroic action figure to loveable oaf. Regardless of the context, that man can deliver, and so can the pentatonic scale!

This section features some two-note and three-note-per-string pentatonic shred exercises that break away from the mundane. The first exercise uses shape one and three of G Minor Pentatonic. It ascends and descends using five-note groupings in 1/16th notes.

Example 1h:

Now we will combine the techniques of alternate picking, economy picking and legato to create this cool D Minor Pentatonic lick in four-note groupings.

Switching between the two different picking techniques is tricky, but the work done here will prepare you for any complex musical situation that might arise.

Example 1i:

In the next exercise you'll shift through the A Minor Pentatonic scale in multiple positions with repetitive six-note groupings.

This exercise builds coordination and dexterity, as well as giving you an unorthodox "circular" shredding approach to explore.

DISCLAIMER: Pay close attention to the 7/8 bars! They are doozies!

Example 1j:

Example 1k is similar to the previous exercise. You'll shift through multiple positions of the A Minor Pentatonic scale, but this time in sexy five-note groupings.

This shredding style, combined with the ascending position shifts, is a go-to trademark of Paul Gilbert and can be heard in quite a few Mr Big and Racer X songs.

Example 1k:

Now move on to Example 1l, where you'll play a three-note-per-string G Major Pentatonic scale idea with a triplet tremolo feel.

The combination of triplets and three-note-per-string pentatonics helps to improve your timing and finger stretching, as well as getting you shredding in a diagonal motion.

Example 1l:

In the final exercise of this section, you'll use the Hirajoshi Pentatonic scale (1 2 b3 5 b6). This scale has made frequent appearances in songs by Trivium and Cacophony.

You'll progress through the scale diagonally across multiple positions using six-note groupings. It shows you that shredding patterns don't need to contain the same number of notes from one string to the next.

Example 1m:

Diatonic & Harmonic Shreds… Incoming blisters!

Diatonic and harmonic scales are an absolute must for heavy metal guitarists. In this section we're going to look at multiple ways to use three-note-per-string patterns in cool shreds and sequences.

The first drill addresses the most common diatonic three-note-per-string shapes. The triplet pulse and string change emphasis means that this exercise is similar to Paul Gilbert's and Buckethead's approach. So, if you wanna be cool like those dudes, this is a great place to start.

Side Note: I am aware that I bring up Paul Gilbert a lot. I am a huge fanboy and think he is an absolute god when it comes to shredding! Sorry-not-sorry lol #livingmybestlife

Example 1n:

The next exercise is a neoclassical-style four-note grouping in the key of A minor. This approach is a less orthodox way of playing the standard three-note-per-string shapes, as it has a 1/16th note pulse and even four-note groupings. The clichéd neo-classical groupings make this an excellent exercise to improve your finger independence and synchronicity.

Example 1o:

Here's another delightful, neoclassical picking sequence using the E Harmonic Minor scale. I've taken inspiration from a four-note grouping and position shift method I discovered many years ago when I was learning the Yngwie Malmsteen classic *Magic Mirror*.

Shredding with multiple position shifts requires you to stay "visually" on top of your playing. In other words, your eye needs to be one step ahead of your fretting hand. Practice this at a reasonable bpm without going too over the top. As you build speed, you'll need to anticipate the position shifts before they happen.

Example 1p:

The final exercise in this section uses the D# Altered Dominant bb7 scale, which is the seventh mode of E Harmonic Minor. It begins with a standard ascent and resolves with a descending four-note arpeggio sequence across two strings.

This is a particularly complex sequence as the first two bars are made of strange note groupings in each bar (4, 1, 5, 3 and 3). Getting comfortable with sequences like this will prepare you for a lifetime of silly and questionable string changes and note groupings. It may also encourage you to be a bit more adventurous when composing your own shred sequences.

Example 1q:

Picking with Arpeggios

People often associate arpeggios with sweeping (which we'll get to in Chapter Three), but in the next few exercises I'm going to show you how to use arpeggios in a different way.

In the first exercise you'll combine three-string arpeggio triads that ascend diatonically through the key of E major, followed by descending mini-shreds, with notes from the diatonic scale.

This exercise helps you master fast string changes in a 1/16th note sequence. It's also provides an alternative to diatonic and pentatonic scales as ways to create fast shred dynamics in your solos.

Example 1r:

Now move on to Example 1s, where you'll see a similar idea that's now played using five-string arpeggio triads.

Example 1s:

Example 1t teaches you to play through multiple stacked Sus2 arpeggios, as well as how to add a double pick on each note. The constant stacking of fifth intervals gives this exercise a somewhat futuristic, spacey sound, reminiscent of players like Steve Vai, Andy Summers and Tosin Abasi.

Double picking each note of the arpeggios requires control and tight right hand/left hand synchronisation. What makes this exercise particularly interesting is that the fretting hand is moving in 1/8th notes while the picking hand is picking 1/16ths – which is pretty groovy if you ask me. *smug eyebrows*

Example 1t:

Now play Example 1u. This exercise moves through diatonic ninth arpeggios in G Major over a few bars of 7/8. The exercise was inspired by the arpeggiated riff in Periphery's technical masterpiece *Marigold*.

Playing over odd meters is a delightful cocktail of challenging concentration and fun. You'll need to focus on clean string changing and play the entire sequence with strict alternate picking.

Example 1u:

Example 1v takes the ideas explored above but adds a string skip... just for fun!

Example 1v:

Stutter Picking

In the final section of this chapter we're going to look at a concept I call *stutter shreds*. I've seen players like Marty Friedman and Dimebag Darrel use this idea to add pauses or stutters in their solos without slowing down their picking hand. They're great for making runs and sequences feel like they're at a stand-still.

In the first exercise you'll take the most common D Minor Pentatonic box shape, but add a triplet stutter at the beginning of each nine-note triplet grouping. The stutter adds a cool bounce to an otherwise linear shred passage.

The tricky part is that you have to combine and synchronise the picking hand (which plays six triplets per bar) with the fretting hand (which essentially moves from 1/8 notes to two triplets, twice per bar). This means that your hands aren't moving at the same speed.

Example 1w:

Now move on to Example 1x, where you'll apply these concepts to the A Lydian Hirajoshi Pentatonic shape.

Example 1x:

The next exercise uses the stuttering pentatonic idea over a B Mixolydian pentatonic shape.

Example 1y:

Finally, let's look at how to use the stutter shred technique with a three-note-per-string shape. To make things exotic and interesting I've chosen the A Hungarian Minor scale spanning three octaves.

This exercise is a creative way to approach diagonal-shaped lead passages, but it is important to synchronise your picking and fretting hand as the timing and emphasis can often differ between the two.

Example 1z:

A Gentleman's Conclusion to Picking

We've looked at some pretty cool ideas in this section, but how can you use them? Well, go and get your hands dirty and actually *try* using some of these weird and whacky concepts in your own solos. Change up the scales, keys or arpeggios. Once the seed is planted it's up to you find the sounds you like.

I've mentioned in all my books (and to many students over the years) the importance of "finding your own voice" on the guitar, so put in the work, get creative and set your sights on conquering the world!

If that's not for you, you can always become an Instagram sensation by adding "metal" guitar vibes to Ariana Grande tunes…

Actually, when I say it out loud that's a terrific idea. I should totally do it.

Chapter Two: Legato for Self Defence

The term "legato" originates from the Italian word for "smooth" or "slurred together". Many shred purists will vow to pick absolutely every note, and consider hammer-ons and pull-offs to be a shortcut "peasant's technique"! I'm here to tell you that some well-placed legato can be exactly what the doctor ordered.

In this chapter we're going to delve into some crazy legato exercises ranging from warm-ups to melodic legato arpeggios and exotic scales.

Warm-up Legato

In this section we'll be looking mainly at chromatic and whole tone scales as a means of strengthening legato articulation and finger independence.

Disclaimer: Whole tone and chromatic scales sound awful 99% of the time. Please don't practice any of the following exercises in the hope of romancing a loved one. The best case scenario is that your atonal efforts will be greeted with a sad pity clap.

Instead, please learn *Your Body is a Wonderland* by John Mayer if your date night is coming up – you'll appear much more attractive and sensitive. If this turns into successful romantic advice, feel free to send me a muffin basket.

In the first exercise you'll use all four fingers to play a chromatic sequence. The alternating finger combinations will show you which finger relationships need strengthening.

Example 2a:

The next example uses chromatics and different finger combinations to strengthen legato technique and finger independence.

Example 2b:

In a similar vein to Examples 2a and 2b, the next exercise involves chromatic legato with all four fingers. This time, however, each string has five-note groupings. Be wary of the 7/8 bars occurring every second measure.

Example 2c:

Now here's a three-note-per-string chromatic exercise.

The descent from bar three onwards may prove challenging, especially if you have weak pinky or have issues with stretching your fretting hand. Drop the bpm of your metronome if you're struggling, but do persevere!

This exercise helps build your pinky strength and develop the kind of stretching needed to play the most ridiculous of Dimebag and Judas Priest licks.

Example 2d:

The final exercise in this section uses the B Whole Tone scale. Again, I've chosen five-note groupings for their lack of predictability and the jazz fusion vibe that comes with it.

Try stick with the index, middle and pinky for the whole exercise. Concentrate on the odd groupings and the clarity of the hammer-ons and pull-offs played by the pinky.

Example 2e:

Badass Pentatonic Legato

The thought of combing pentatonic ideas with legato might remind you of the likes of Kirk Hammett, Randy Rhoads and Ace Frehley, but pentatonics can be mysterious and awesome; unpredictable, yet sexy! Imagine late 90s heartthrob David Boreanaz as a scale (he played Angel in *Buffy The Vampire Slayer)*. Unexpected, but brooding.

In this section you'll explore interesting ways to combine pentatonics and legato, with interesting picking emphasis and unorthodox three-note-per-string shapes.

In the first exercise, we'll look at a seemingly predictable Minor Pentatonic sequence, but by doubling the first note in each four-note grouping we'll add an interesting emphasis to your phrasing to give it a Dimebagesque quality.

Example 2f:

Now move on to Example 2g, where you'll change from vertical, two-note-per-string shapes, to a diagonal pattern that uses a combination of two- and four-notes per string. The grouping and accent emphasis will change from two notes to six notes on the string changes.

This exercise will not only help you get creative with interesting notes groupings, it will also improve your four fingered legato strength and technique.

Example 2g:

Next, move on to this D Minor Pentatonic lick that combines three-note-per-string legato with a neo-classical six-note motif.

I first heard this idea in the Yngwie Malmsteen song *Fire & Ice*... and if I know Yngzy-J, he probably took some influence from Paganini, Vivaldi and Bach.

Example 2h:

In the next exercise, you'll ascend through a Hirajoshi scale using only your index and middle fingers, and create a spooky trilling sound. You can hear this idea used by Alex Skolnick in the solo of *Practice What You Preach* by Testament at around the 3:05 mark.

This is a great way to build finger strength and develop the relationship between your index and middle fingers. It also shows that interesting and colourful melodies can be played with just two fingers!

Example 2i:

Next, we'll play the G Mixolydian Pentatonic scale (G B C D F) across six strings with sliding positions shifts and legato.

This exercise moves in a diagonal manner instead of the usual vertical, pentatonic box shape. This will hopefully spawn some creativity and show you that minor, Mixolydian and Hirajoshi pentatonics can be played in some really interesting ways!

Example 2j:

In Example 2k you'll use similar concepts, but this time with the Bb Lydian Hirajoshi Pentatonic scale (Bb D E F A).

Example 2k:

Deadly Diatonic Legato

Whether I'm writing a solo or improvising off the cuff, I tend to gravitate towards legato, especially when I'm playing diatonic three-note-per-string passages.

As a personal preference, I have always liked the way legato sounds more than picking. But we all know that in some cases you just *have* to pick!

The thing I really love about three-note-per-string legato is the sound of the notes bleeding into one another, which can combine elements of chaos, endlessness and an unhinged delivery. If you listen to players like Joe Satriani, Guthrie Govan, Nuno Bettencourt and Alex Skolnick (to name a few), you can hear some really creative ways to get diatonic legato to sound cool and fresh.

In this first exercise, we will use an Alex Skolnick-style position shift legato with the F# Minor scale. The combination of rolling legato, slides and position shifts make an otherwise linear diatonic passage sound awesome.

With enough repetition, this exercise will severely increase your legato gains as you have play *eight* legato notes per pick!

Example 2l:

In Example 2m you'll use Satriani-esque rolls, slides and legato to combine two three-note-per-string shapes. It contains five-note groupings in each position shift, as well as *ten* legato notes per pick!

Example 2m:

Next, I've combined the G Major three-note-per-string shape with the B Phrygian shape and more five-note groupings. Be wary of the reoccurring 7/8 bars too!

This exercise will not only help develop your ability to play legato in five-note groupings, it's also heavily reliant on your pinky finger. As the weakest and lamest of the finger family, you can never overdo isolated pinky practice or exercises that emphasise and encourage its use.

Example 2n:

In the next exercise, we'll play diatonic three-note-per-string legato with string skips. These have a great sound as certain intervals and parts of the scale have been omitted, which creates the inference of an arpeggio.

You can hear players like Nuno Bettencourt and Paul Gilbert use this idea in countless solos. You can also hear this exact legato technique at the beginning of the brief, yet awesome solo from Journey's *Don't Stop Believing*.

Example 2o:

Legato Arpeggios... Is That Even a Thing?!

For many guitarists the notion of "legato arpeggios" seems like a pretty farfetched concept. The common thought process would be "you either sweep an arpeggio or pick through it" And, to be fair, this is a fairly straight forward deduction. But bear with me as I wish to take you on an excellent adventure and open your mind!

A few years ago, I started listening to Sylosis. Josh Middleton, the band's lead guitarist and main songwriter, has a playing style and a way of phrasing his leads that absolutely blew me away. His use of legato in arpeggios was like nothing I'd ever heard before and this inspired me to explore the concept a little further.

Most exercises in this section will be based around string skipped "7th" arpeggios.

Let's look at a way to combine arpeggios in three octaves with hammer-ons, slides and position shifts. This will not only give you some different ways to approach these arpeggios, it will also help you to cover the fretboard diagonally while increasing your pinky strength and dexterity.

Example 2p:

In the next example you'll combine string skipping and legato to create a descending diminished arpeggio sequence that resolves with an ascending chromatic idea.

The string skipping requires that you concentrate on your picking, as well as the difficult challenge of the six-fret stretch. It's also worth mentioning that there are no pull-offs in this exercise, so you can use it to build your hammer-on technique gains.

Example 2q:

Now let's play multiple seventh arpeggios in a pleasant melodic sequence.

As in the previous example, this exercise contains string-skipped legato phrases that require some extra brain power for your picking and fretting hand. With practice, you'll master some new arpeggio shapes for your arsenal, as well as a firmer grasp on string-skipped legato playing.

Example 2r:

Next, we'll take influence from hair metal gods Nuno Bettencourt and Paul Gilbert to play a complex string-skipped arpeggio lick containing legato and fast triplets. Use this exercise to drill the fundamentals of string skipping and pinky strength to build your legato technique.

Example 2s:

Messaen Diminished & Melodic Minor Legato

Because I'm a weirdo and like strange scales, I felt it was only fitting that I include some Melodic Minor and Messaen Diminished scales… because this is *my* book, not yours! #diva.

These two scales sound particularly weird and freaky when played with legato and odd note groupings, and they're a great place to start if you want to add some Allan Holdsworth style ideas to your playing.

In the first exercise we'll use a G Melodic Minor three-note-per-string shape and ascend through it with a slippery five-note grouping. This will help develop your five-note legato technique and it also works well over min(Maj7) chords when they arise.

Example 2t:

In Example 2u we'll use a combination of legato and slides to ascend and descend through a Messaen-style G# Diminished Half-Whole scale. This kind of legato lick can be played over a diminished chord or a III7 chord beginning from the major 3rd. It's also a great way to practice diagonal legato with four notes per string.

Example 2u:

Now move on to Example 2w where we'll explore the G# diminished scale further, this time using a combination of legato, slides and six-note groupings.

Example 2v:

Hammer-ons From Nowhere

Once upon a time I discovered Greg Howe and was immediately perplexed by his "hammer-ons from nowhere" technique. Put simply, this is hammering on to a new string that hasn't been picked. This creates a cool shortcut way to access extra notes that could have only been played with a complex picking pattern.

In this section all of the hammer-ons-from-nowhere licks will be based around diatonic runs and sequences to get you used to the technique in a familiar melodic setting.

In the first exercise, we'll ascend through an A Aeolian three-note-per-string shape using a more traditional legato approach, but also add a few hammer-ons from nowhere. Pay close attention to the notation and notice where the change to a new string is hammered instead of picked.

Example 2w:

Now use a similar approach to descend through C Ionian.

Example 2x:

Let's try it with the B Minor Blues Scale.

Example 2y:

This final exercise combines ascending and descending hammer-ons from nowhere and works its way through every position of G Major.

Example 2z:

Smoother & Weirder: A Smooth Summation

I believe legato to be one of the most important and expressive techniques for soloing and I seem to gravitate towards it much more than picking. That said, a tasteful combination of the two will make you a well-rounded and versatile player.

Then again, maybe there's nothing *sexy* about being "well-rounded" and "versatile"! If you really want to turn heads, exotic legato, arpeggios, and hammer-ons-from-nowhere can take your legato from "I just do hammer-ons when I should be picking" to next-level techniques that bring a unique and unusual flavour to the table.

Your homework is to work through all the legato exercises, experiment by adding them into your own licks, then incorporate these ideas into your solos and compositions.

Chapter Three: Arpeggios and Crazy Sweeps

Sweeping has always been a "just because you can, doesn't mean you should" technique for me. I think it's best used to add a brief moment of flair and speed, rather than for lengthy periods of swept arpeggio sequences, but that's just my opinion.

I think the master of tasteful sweeps is Alex Skolnick of Testament. I've always loved how Alex will place a cheeky sweep here and there, but only as a means to add a sensual garnish to his solos.

On the flipside of that coin are players like Jason Becker, Yngwie Malmsteen and Jason Richardson who will sweep at you till your face melts – which can be charming at times but may grate after a while.

That said, getting this technique under your belt (along with some musical context to apply it), helps you to tackle even the toughest sweeps as and when they arise.

Warm-up Nonsense Sweeps

Let's begin by covering some warm-ups and arpeggio fundamentals, just to get your brain and fingers ready for some challenging sweeps. Some of these exercises are not what you'd call "pleasing to the ear", but bear with me, I promise you'll see fruitful results if you put in the work.

In the first example you'll see multiple inversions of a few three-note triad arpeggio sweeps played across two strings. This is a relatively simple idea and only requires a downward sweeping motion. It's an excellent warm-up to get your sweeping and fretting hands in sync.

Example 3a:

The next idea is a common sweeping motion that moves across all six strings. However (plot twist!) you're only going to play dead, muted notes, so you can focus solely on your picking hand's direction without any melodic distractions.

Each sweep is divided into four-note groups of three ascending and one descending. This exercise helps train you to tackle sudden, mid-sweep, picking direction changes, as well as teaching you to sweep gradually through the strings, instead of just playing one big arpeggio. Pay close attention to the picking directions in the diagram before you play!

Example 3b:

Now use the sweeping motion you've developed to work through stacked, three-string, tritone chord shapes.

Example 3c:

To finish this section, the final example uses ascending tritone arpeggios played with four-fingered chord shapes. The picking directions are similar to examples 3b and 3c, but every third arpeggio has a picking variation on the fourth note that helps you rearrange your wrist and sweep picking direction.

Example 3d:

Upgrade Your Three-String Sweeps

The humble three-string sweep is the best "look at me" technique for the noob shredders of the world, but it shouldn't be shunned for its simplicity. Getting a good grasp of some three-string arpeggio sweeps is always useful because they come up time and time again. If you come across them used in a brief, tasteful manner, or in a long sequence of arpeggios, this section will get you be prepared to tackle them with valour.

Let's start with a relatively simple idea that focuses on descending three-string sweeps. As a standalone skill or compositional technique, they are used far less in solos than their ascending counterparts, and over the years I've found that they are often rushed or played sloppily by many players.

Pay close attention to the picking directions!

Example 3e:

Next we'll look at a Black Metal influenced arpeggio sequence that switches between D Harmonic and D Natural minor. This is a great exercise to get your three-string sweep arpeggio chops together, but has the added bonus of occurring over an interesting, non-vanilla chord progression. Let's just say it might be appropriate to get your black and white face paint out!

Example 3f:

The next idea uses three-string 7th arpeggios in two positions to gradually work through the diatonic chords of G Major. This is an excellent exercise to help develop the skill of position shifts to different inversions of the same arpeggio and means you can create movement without changing chord.

Example 3g:

Now play through the three-string arpeggios shown below to work your way through all the diatonic chords of A Melodic Minor.

Example 3h:

Warning: Incoming personal story

In about 2013-ish I had a student who was obsessed with Nevermore. Upon learning their tunes, I fell in love with the band and Jeff Loomis' insane, evil playing style. I was particularly drawn to his incorporation of the Phrygian Dominant mode and diminished arpeggios in his solos.

Taking inspiration from the solo in Nevermore's *Born*, I've put together a three-string arpeggio sequence that uses Jeff's signature, inverse, diminished sweep approach. This will give you some new directions and approaches to use with diminished sweeps. It's so easy to get caught playing an idea and moving it up three frets. We've all done it, but Jeff taught me how to make it fresh and sassy!

Example 3i:

In the next exercise you'll combine swept, three-string, suspended 2nd chord shapes with basic triads. This adds the 9th of the scale without sounding too linear.

This is an especially cool concept as the arpeggios ascend and descend in different ways and can be used to cover six strings. These multiple "mini-sweeps" create an interesting dynamic in your playing and break up the common approach of playing long boring triads or obscenely complicated arpeggios.

Example 3j:

Brace yourself! In the next exercise you're going to work through multiple ninth arpeggios in five-note groupings, to create an extensive arpeggio sequence.

A ninth arpeggio is made up of the 1st, 3rd, 5th, 7th and 9th of a chord, so can naturally form five-note groupings. Ninth arpeggios create a contrast to triads or seventh arpeggios and, of course, the odd numbered grouping can be a simple way to make your solos sound less predictable.

Example 3k:

Level Up Your Five-String Sweeps

When I first learned how to sweep five-string arpeggios I thought, "Yeah, I've arrived… I'm a man now!" To me, it was essentially the guitar equivalent of being able to find firewood, create shelter, and stave off bear attacks – all while feeling at home in the wilderness. In this deluded fantasy I imagined myself to have an excellent beard.

My existential crisis aside, learning to put these arpeggios into my solos and confidently tackle them in covers was crucial to my development as a guitarist.

In my first book, *Ultimate Shred Machine* I covered some pretty basic arpeggio stuff, so I'm going to assume you're up for learning some outlandish five-string sweep sequences. If you haven't read it, you're in for a terrifying treat.

Let's kick off with this Black Metal style arpeggio sequence that combines five-string and three-string triads. Jumping between different length arpeggios breaks up the predictability of arpeggiated sequences by varying the rhythm and accents.

Example 3l:

The next example contains a few five-string triad arpeggios in D Major that ascend and descend one full octave.

Pay close attention to the slides and look where you're going to move to a few notes before the end of the ascending part of the arpeggio. This will improve your hand-eye coordination, as well as help you to take more risks with how far you slide.

Example 3m:

Now you'll play a combination of ascending major and minor triads that descend in either an augmented or diminished fashion. There's a degree of chromaticism in this exercise that might spawn some cool ideas for your own chromatic, spooky arpeggio sequences.

Example 3n:

In the next exercise you'll work through some complex ninth arpeggios in the key of C Minor. You'll be working across five-strings, three of which have hammer-ons, which will require your sweeping hand to slow down so that your fretting hand can catch up.

Learning to sweep seventh and ninth arpeggios is excellent for hand synchronicity practice, but comes with the added bonus of expanding your soloing and arpeggio vocabulary.

Example 3o:

Change Your Six-String Sweep Game

The six-string sweep is often omitted from a guitarist's arsenal as the arpeggio shapes themselves are not conventionally "comfy". This has led to an abundance of three- and five-stringed arpeggios played all over the place, leaving the poor six-string arpeggio to be used much as Metapod in the original Pokémon Gameboy game.

To right this wrong *raises index finger*, I've put together some new exercises that are way cooler and more difficult than the ones in *Ultimate Shred Machine*! In this section you'll see six-string arpeggios that encompass triads, sevenths, elevenths, thirteenths and even some suspended notes! Woah!

In the first exercise there's a combination of six-string triad arpeggios and paired four-string sus2 arpeggios. This is a cool way to drift from triads to something less predictable. It also serves as a great exercise for drifting between six-string and four-string sweeps for your picking hand.

Example 3p:

Next you'll see major and minor seventh arpeggios spanning three octaves with multiple position shifts. This is a great way to play swept arpeggios in a horizontal manner, as well as breaking the mould of typical arpeggio shapes and voicings.

Example 3q:

The following example involves stacked sus2 arpeggios that create a superimposed 11th arpeggio sound.

Again, these arpeggios help you sweep less predictably, as well as showing you how to incorporate some sophisticated 11th arpeggios into your soloing vocabulary.

Example 3r:

In Example 3s you'll sweep though familiar stacked suspended shapes to create a variety of complex 13th arpeggios. These shapes are inspired by the crazy sequences seen in the Satriani masterpiece *Mystical Potato Groove Thing*.

Example 3s:

Building Sweeps

It's easy to think of a sweep as just an arpeggio played up or down in its entirety. My issue with this is the lack of variance in melodic direction, as well as it being a waste of the tension that could be built by not giving your audience the full big-arpeggio payoff. So, in this section we'll explore arpeggios that build gradually.

In the first exercise you'll gradually work through multiple chunks of a B Augmented arpeggio, three strings at a time.

This concept works perfectly over BAug, D#Aug and GAug chords and can also be played in a Phrygian Dominant context in the keys of B, D# and G.

Pay close attention to where each triplet ends and stay mindful of the picking directions.

Example 3t:

Let's take that B Augmented arpeggio but add a hammer-on in each position to create an augmented arpeggio that builds through four-note groupings in each position.

Example 3u:

In the next example, we'll again build through a B Augmented arpeggio but this time in six-note groupings while adding slightly more complex position shifts.

Example 3v:

The next sequence of six-string arpeggios descends in multiple four-note groupings.

These arpeggios are just major and minor triads but this grouping and sweeping approach can also be applied to seventh, diminished and augmented arpeggios.

Example 3w:

In the next exercise, you'll work through a few different positions of a diminished arpeggio, swept in five- and seven-note groupings. This approach breaks up the monotony of four-note and three-note groupings and makes your arpeggio phrases less predictable.

Note that the combinations of multiple odd-numbered groupings are written with the measures changing from 4/4 to 3/4 every bar.

Example 3x:

Next we'll use similar groupings and sweep patterns, but this time play augmented arpeggios. Once again, the time signature changes from 4/4 to 3/4 every bar.

Example 3y:

Finally, let's work through a simple chord progression but use a four-note grouping method to gradually sweep through major and minor triad arpeggios.

This is a cool way to work through an arpeggio shape in an incremental manner, especially if you want to draw it out for more than half a bar. It sounds much more interesting than just repeatedly going up and down a big arpeggio in exactly the same way to fill out the bar before the chord changes.

Once you are comfortable with this concept, put together your own simple chord progression and use major and minor triad arpeggios with this gradual sweeping method.

Example 3z:

Revenge of the Janitor: Sweeps & Reflections

Sweep arpeggios should be like snowflakes… no two the same. Many great players get the fundamentals of sweeping down, only to get stuck using the same vanilla major, minor and diminished shapes they learnt decades ago.

I hope that after you've studied this chapter, your sweep vocabulary will become more sophisticated, whether by the incorporation of stacked suspended arpeggios, the use of major and minor 13ths, gradually building sweep patterns, or even just by throwing in the occasional cheeky augmented arpeggio (lord knows I do!)

Get creative and *get out of that rut!* I know many players who say, "I hate sweeping" or "it sounds like a trick!" but it can be an enjoyable technique, with subtle merit and distinctive flavour.

If you are willing to put in the time, take melodic risks, and familiarise yourself with some not-so-straightforward arpeggio shapes, I promise there'll be a situation at some point in your life where you'll play a delicious sweep and be all like, "Yeah! That was the right move."

Chapter Four: Outlandish Tapping

Could any guitar technique be cooler than tapping? Surely not!

Eddie Van Halen made a career out of being "that tapping guy" and hats off to him. Me, personally? I love a cheeky tap. Sometimes a tapped sequence can create a wonderfully interesting effect that you couldn't otherwise get from legato or string skips.

In this chapter you're going to master some tapping warm-ups, crazy creative exercises, and even learn how to get sensual with your tapping finger!

Warm-up Taps

In this first section we'll devote some time to tapping warm-ups and building the fundamentals that'll prepare you for the crazy whizz-bizz that will follow later in the chapter.

The first example uses a chromatic, three-note pattern with the tapping hand mirroring the fretting hand three frets higher.

Mastering this coordination will help you to divide your attention between your hands and build their synchronicity.

Example 4a:

In the next exercise you'll use three fingers on the fretting hand to play rolling chromatic legato lines and combine them with a single tap on the picking hand. The exercise will descend and ascend using six- and four-note groupings.

This might be tricky at first, but it quickly becomes more predictable to play. In this exercise you'll be forced to think outside the box and concentrate on oddly placed taps that fall mid-sequence.

Example 4b:

Now move on to Example 4c. Staying within the theme of tapped chromatics, this exercise combines four-note legato patterns in the fretting hand with two rolling tapped fingers on the picking hand. With persistence this exercise will build your fretting hand strength and give you more exposure to multi-fingered tapping.

Disclaimer: This is a rather repugnant sounding exercise, so you may want to turn your amp down, especially if you're within earshot of anyone you're trying to impress romantically.

Example 4c:

Example 4d once again uses an amalgamation of chromatic scales and tapped notes. In this instance, the fretting hand uses just two fingers, but with many shifts and slides.

Example 4d:

Pentatonic Taps for Snazzy Ladies & Gentleman

In this section you'll learn to turn the otherwise humble and bland minor pentatonic scale into something snazzy and awesome. Of course, this is achieved by adding some cheeky taps. The great thing about adding taps to pentatonics is that they sound rather snazzy and make you look like a charismatic gangsta on stage.

In this example you'll play the F Minor Pentatonic in two different octaves using the same scale shape. This may sound impossible but is done by mirroring the tapping hand to create somewhat of an octave delay.

Example 4e:

Next, we'll take this idea and do something similar with the G Lydian Hirajoshi Pentatonic scale across two octaves.

Example 4f:

Now play through this tapped A Mixolydian Pentatonic idea, once again using the mirroring technique seen above.

Example 4g:

Here you'll see the A Minor Pentatonic played from box shape one and ascending with string skips and taps from shape two. Then we descend through box shape two adding strings skips and taps from shape three.

With practice, the following exercise will help you master tapped string skips and fast position shifts. This is extremely helpful if you want to incorporate lengthy, intervallic-sounding tapped sequences into your solos.

Example 4h:

Finally, let's combine a D Minor Pentatonic three-note-per-string shape with taps and string skips. Be wary of the 7/8 measures through the exercise.

You may have seen this tapped pentatonic approach used by players like Guthrie Govan, Synyster Gates, Rusty Cooley, and those cheeky young whippersnappers from Polyphia. It will help you to break out of the traditional two-note-per-string pentatonic box, with the added bonus of working on stretched legato shapes and honing your dexterity.

Example 4i:

Diabolic Diatonic Taps

In this section, you'll combine taps with diatonic scales to create interesting and exciting passages. You'll need to have confidence with the three-note-per-string legato technique, as this will get more complicated when you add some crazy whizz-bizz tapping ideas.

The first exercise combines taps with ascending and descending rolls. You'll essentially use both the E Ionian and the C# Aeolian three-note-per-string shape across all six strings.

This concept could be moved to any pair of diatonic three-note-per-string scale shapes.

Example 4j:

Now things get more complicated as we add more legato with a second tapping finger. This creates a "rolling effect" in your tapping hand that we're normally only used to hearing from fretting hand legato.

For most of this exercise your fretting hand only holds one note, so you can direct most of your attention to the multi-fingered tapping technique.

Example 4k:

In Example 4l you'll play through a diatonic F# minor sequence with two tapping fingers across three octaves. The two fingered tapping style is reminiscent of players like Guthrie Govan, Synyster Gates and Chris Broderick.

This exercise will require a great deal of dedication and patience to master. The main challenge is developing the synchronisation between the three-note-per-string fretting hand and the two tapping hand fingers.

Once you have this skill in your arsenal you can pull out some pretty crazy taps, and it's always good to have the option of a second tapping finger should you need it!

Example 4l:

Line 1 TAB: 2 4 5 7 9 7 5 4 2 4 5 9 10 9 5 4 | 2 4 5 7 9 7 5 4 2 4 5 9 11 9 5 4

Line 2 TAB: 4 6 7 9 11 9 7 6 4 6 7 11 12 11 7 6 | 4 6 7 9 11 9 7 6 4 6 7 11 13 11 7 6

Line 3 TAB: 7 9 10 12 14 12 10 9 7 9 10 14 15 14 10 9 | 7 9 10 12 14 12 10 9 7 9 10 14 16 14 10 9

Exotic Taps (Let's Get Sassy)

I'm a gentleman who loves a curve ball. You might be thinking: "Adding taps to pentatonics and diatonic scales… yawn, Chris! Give me a challenge!" Well, hopefully this next section is what you've been waiting for.

We're going to take the diatonic and pentatonic ideas we've studied so far and use them to create some interesting patterns with some exotic scales – such as the Phrygian Dominant, Hungarian Minor and Diminished Whole-Half.

We'll begin with an E Phrygian Dominant scale and a combination of legato and double taps.

The double tap was a signature technique of Randy Rhoads and can be heard in Kirk Hammett's *Wherever I May Roam* solo which heavily influenced this lick.

Example 4m:

Now try a similar idea with a G# Diminished scale shape run with double taps.

Example 4n:

In the next exercise, you'll play through the A Hungarian Minor scale with added tapped coolness and charisma.

Pay close attention to the formations that ascend and descend every second string after each tap. This pattern can be used with any three-note-per-string shape and will encourage less linear tapping and more position shifts.

Example 4o:

Now we'll play a combination of legato and taps working through the C# Diminished Half-Whole scale. The premise is relatively simple in that you ascend through a three-note-per-string scale with an added tap, and descend via a string-skipped diminished tapped arpeggio.

This kind of lick would work really well over a C#dim7, Edim7, Gdim7 or A#dim7 chord, as the scale outlines the chord tones of each one. It would also work wonderfully in a D Harmonic minor or A Phrygian Dominant setting, whenever an A7 chord makes an appearance.

Example 4p:

Advanced Tapped Arpeggios

Sometimes, when I'm writing a solo or a passage of melody, I might hear a sequence of arpeggios in my head. I'll sit down to pick or sweep through them, and it'll either not quite fit the music or not sound like what's in my head. Luckily, there's more than two ways to play an arpeggio. I'm talking of course about tapped arpeggios.

If I didn't mention it in *Ultimate Shred Machine*, playing multiple notes of an arpeggio on three different strings - or one full triad on one string (with the help of a tap, of course) will still have the same melodic content, but have a different tonal or timbral quality. In the next section of this chapter you'll be learning some pretty crazy tapped arpeggio sequences.

In the first example you'll see string skipped, seventh arpeggios with taps on the 5th, 3rd and 1st string. Every two bars will show a combination of two arpeggios creating a superimposed 9th arpeggio effect.

Example 4q:

Now tackle Example 4r, where you'll play an extensive BAug arpeggio with taps across all six strings.

This exercise not only sounds freaky and awesome, but has the added bonus of working over D#Aug and GAug chords as well. If you're feeling particularly adventurous, augmented arpeggios of all varieties will sound great over a dominant chord, whether it's in a Harmonic Minor/Phrygian Dominant or Melodic Minor/Hindu Mixolydian situation.

Example 4r:

In the next exercise, you'll play through some Josh Middleton style string skipped arpeggios with the addition of taps. Throughout this sequence, pay close attention to how the fretting hand legato changes direction each string, on every second tap.

Once you're playing sequences like this confidently, they may serve as a compositional tool, or just as a means to play an arpeggio in a less linear manner.

Example 4s:

Now move on to play Example 4t, where you'll use a combination of power chord shapes and sliding taps to create a pleasing ninth arpeggio sequence. This exercise could be played in a distorted or clean context. If it spurs inspiration, see if you can write your own "ninthy" (a word I just made up) chord, slide-tapped sequence.

Example 4t:

Next, play through Example 4u, where you'll play a sequence of "mirroring" two octave power chords to create the inference of suspended 2nd arpeggios. Also be mindful that this exercise uses a 7/8 time signature.

The concept of "tapped arpeggio mirroring" was something I saw Guthrie Govan do as he played a diminished arpeggio on his fretting hand, then mimicked the exact sequence shortly after on his tapping hand three frets up.

Musically speaking, this kind of arpeggio has a very futuristic, spacey sound. This could be attributed to the placement and intervals of the tap pull offs, as well as the complete absence of major and minor thirds.

Example 4u:

In the next example you'll use Nuno Bettencourt's signature tapped arpeggio approach to work through a chord sequence in D Major. This approach can most notably be seen in the Extreme classic *Get the Funk Out*.

This approach is an excellent alternative to straight sweeps or the Eddie Van Halen/Randy Rhoads approach of one-string triads. Have fun with this exercise and when you feel confident, try to put together a short sequence of arpeggios of your own!

Example 4v:

Finally, move on to Example 4w, where you'll play through a lengthy diminished arpeggio sequence. It will essentially be a combination of legato, string-skipped arpeggios and double taps.

This exercise takes inspiration from the great Randy Rhoads and repeatedly capitalises on his double tapped arpeggio approach. You can hear this concept being perfectly executed in the Ozzy Osbourne classic *Flying High Again*.

With enough patience, this exercise will increase your double tap clarity and also aid in string skipped arpeggios with taps. Do be mindful of the subdivisions drifting from triplet 1/16ths to regular 1/16ths.

Example 4w:

Expressive Taps: How to Tap... With Your Heart on Your Sleeve

People often think of taps as a pizazzy technique – and due to the way it's been abused by countless players over the years, it's not an unfair assessment. But today's the day that you're going to learn something different! Let's put the speed and flashyness aside for a moment and look at tapping as an expressive technique.

To create a harp-like effect you can strum seventh chords and add tapped scale notes and pull-offs. This will arpeggiate the chord while adding in a few tasty colour tones. I recommend practicing this idea with a clean amp setting, as seventh chords get lost in any distortion.

When you get the hang of this idea, try putting together a simple chord progression and add in some tasteful, melodic taps.

Example 4x:

Next, you'll combine the first shape of A Minor Pentatonic with a powerful bent tap to add an element of emotion while increasing the melodic range of your fretting hand.

Don't try to bend or shake the note with your tapping hand. Do all of the expressive work with your fretting hand. The tapping hand should just hold the fret that is being bent or has vibrato on it.

Example 4y:

In a similar vein, we'll now use the D Lydian Hirajoshi Pentatonic scale, but add an expressive tap on each string. As before, be mindful that all vibrato should come from your fretting hand and not from your tapping hand.

Example 4z:

Tapping Tastefully: When and Why You Should Tap

I will always have a soft spot for tapping. Not only is it flashy, it really helps to expand the range of our melodies.

In *Ultimate Shred Machine* I tried to give you a reasonable grasp of tapping, without too much scary fancy-pants malarkey. In this book, however, we're on a no-holds-barred exploration of weird and whacky sounds designed to get you creative with what could be a somewhat dated technique. As with sweeping, I feel that tapping is in danger of being added to the "just a parlour trick" category, and I genuinely don't believe this should be the case.

With enough dedication and by exploring the exercises in this chapter, you can find a way to get creative, build your confidence, and add a musical flourish to your solos.

Epilogue & Acknowledgments

Wowzer! Four books, done and dusted! To say that I'm proud of myself is a massive understatement. It'd be like saying "monkeys only *slightly* enjoy throwing poo at each other."

Hopefully, the ideas in this book have opened your mind to new sonic possibilities and given you plenty of ammunition to break out of any rut you may find yourself in. The Chris Zoupa "broken record" advice is "practice, experiment and find your sound". Most importantly, make sure you have fun incorporating any new ideas into your playing along the way. If it stops being fun, it's time to mix things up!

I wouldn't have been able to finish this ridiculous undertaking without the push of my students and YouTube community. You all challenge me every day. I'm still learning and working on becoming the best version of myself as a player and person. Thank you.

To amazing publisher and editor duo, Joseph and Tim – you guys are like some sort of literary great uncles. Your constant guidance and support over the past few years has meant the world to me and I'm eternally grateful.

To my bandmates Dean, Andrew and Nick from Teramaze, thanks for the challenging music and amazing opportunity to write with you guys. If it wasn't for the incessant roasting, I would say that this band is a match made in heaven. I know it's corny, but it's just how I feel!

Finally, to my gorgeous little family. Alexi, my special little boy, whose perplexing questions and off-colour humour always catches me off guard.

Andrew Rodriguez (my 11-year-old cat), you're a fat fluffy jerk! Please come home before 9:00pm!

Our most recent addition, Juniper "Juno" Stevenson, you are an adorable little kitten. I just wish you wouldn't attack my feet while I'm asleep.

And lastly, my darling wife, Lucie, thanks for sticking by me all these years and going along with whatever weird undertaking or devious scheme I sign up to. You're a treasure and a sweet woman.

www.ingramcontent.com/pod-product-compliance
Lightning Source LLC
Chambersburg PA
CBHW081433090426
42740CB00017B/3292